Love's Kingdom

A Pastoral Trage-Comedy

With a Short Treatise of the English Stage

by

Richard Flecknoe

with a preface
for the Garland Edition by

Arthur Freeman

Garland Publishing, Inc., New York & London

1973

Copyright © 1973

by Garland Publishing, Inc.

All Rights Reserved

PR
3461
.F4
L6
1973

Library of Congress Cataloging in Publication Data

Flecknoe, Richard, d. 1678?
  Love's kingdom.

  (The English stage: attack and defense, 1577-1730)
  A revision of the author's Love's dominion.
  Reprint of the 1664 ed. printed by R. Wood for the
author, London.
    1. Theater--Great Britain--History. I. Title.
II. Series.
PR3461.F4L6 1973   822'.4   74-170431
ISBN 0-8240-0600-3

Printed in the United States of America

Preface

The "Short Discourse of the English Stage" which Richard Flecknoe prefixes to his rewritten play Love's Kingdom *is perhaps less a defense of theater than an epitome of its history and praise of its past; but both in the "Discourse" and in the play itself is a didactic or prescriptive line characteristic of all Flecknoe's writings for the stage — all but this never acted.* Love's Kingdom *is, as Langbaine pointed out, only a little altered from the author's closet drama,* Love's Dominion *(1654), "written as a Pattern for the* Reformed Stage,*" and dedicated to Cromwell's daughter, Lady Elizabeth Claypole. At the Restoration, shifting sides, Flecknoe obtained the King's leave to have it performed, and its relative failure in some part inspired the more significant discourse, which Langbaine calls "the best thing he has extant."*

Richard Flecknoe himself has of course been immortalized by Andrew Marvell and by Dryden —

PREFACE

priest, poet, and musician, "so thin and meagre that he looked as if he had fed on nothing but consecrated wafers" (Oldys), obsessed with his own verse to the point of mania, and a traveler who ranged from Constantinople to Brazil. He has had his share of qualified admiration, by Genest, Southey, Lamb, and Leslie Stephen (in DNB), and would seem ripe for reappraisal.

*The "Short Discourse" is dedicated to the Marquess of Newcastle (Langbaine remarks that "[Flecknoe's] Acquaintance with the Nobility, was more than with the Muses"). It was reprinted by Hazlitt (1869) and edited by Spingarn (*Critical Essays of the Seventeenth Century, *II, 91-6). The present reprint is prepared from a copy at the British Museum (11775.a.2), with a better title page supplied from a copy at Yale (Beinecke Ij F623 664). The collation is $A^4 B$-G^8. Lowe-Arnott-Robinson 820.*

February, 1973   A. F.

Love's Kingdom.

A

Pastoral Trage-Comedy.

Not as it was Acted at the Theatre near *Lincolns-Inn*, but as it was written, and since corrected

BY

Richard Flecknoe.

With a short Treatise of the *English Stage, &c.* by the same Author.

LONDON,
Printed by R. *Wood* for the Author, 1664.

Licenſed,   April 22.
1664.

Roger L' Eſtrange.

To his Excellence, *William*, Lord Marquess of *Newcastle*.

My Noble Lord,

THe People, *who (as one sayes well) are Judges without Judgement, and Authors without Authority, had condemn'd this* Play *on the Stage, for want of being rightly represented unto them; at which, many noble Persons were so much offended, as I could not in any one Act do it more right, or give them more satisfaction, then by Printing it, to shew its Innocence. As it is, it has had the honour to have been approv'd by most of the better and wiser* **Sort**; *and*

The Epistle Dedicatory.

and if your Excellence but adde unto it your Approbation, I desire no more. It wants much of the Ornament of the Stage, but that by a lively imagination may easily be supplyed: For my part, unless it may be presented as I writ it, and as I intended it, I had rather it shu'd be read then acted, and have the World for Theatre, rather then the Stage.

Having said thus much by way of Prologue, I leave you to the Play, remaining alwayes,

Your Excellencies

Most humble, and most devoted Servant,

Richard Flecknoe.

To the noble Readers.

TO think to write without faults, is to think to peel a *Bulbus* Root to the last Rinde, or sweep an earthen Floor to the last grain of dust; and 'tis here, as in the Mint, where if the Dross exceed not the pure *Or*, it passes for currant Coin. The greatest fault in this kinde of writing, is to erre against Art and *Decorum*, of which I hope this Play is free; who findes fault with the mirth in it, never consider how here with us, mirth in Playes of this kinde is like Alloy in Coin, which though it abases it, yet makes it more passible. For the Rhyme, 'tis more excusable in Pastorals, then in other Playes; and where I leave the Rhyme or numbers, I imagin'd, that as a good Actor was like a good Singer, so a good Play was like a good Song; where 'tis not necessary all notes shu'd be of an equal length. For the Plot 'tis neat and handsome, and the Language soft and gentle, suitable to the persons who speak, neither on the Ground, nor in the Clouds; but just like the Stage, somewhat elevated above the common. In neither, no stifness, and (I hope) no impertinence nor extravagance; into which,

your

To the Reader.

your young writers are apt to run; who whilst they know not well what to do, and are anxious to do enough, most commonly overdo. Those who think it so easie now to make a good Play, will tell me some twenty years hence how hard it is; when they will finde that 'tis not a good Humor or two in a Comedy will do it, (which are good supports 'tis true; but to think they will make a Play, is to think a Pillar or two sufficient to make a House) nor the writing a fine Copy of Verses or two, sufficient to make a Tragedy, or Trage-Comedy; but there must go a *Genius* as well as *Ingenium* to't, with long exercise and experience. But to leave their Playes, and return to ours; if you like it for whom I writ it, I have my end, which was onely in an innocent and harmless way, to divert my self and you.

The

The Persons represented.

THe *Prologue spoken by* Venus *from the Clouds*
   Theotimus, *Loves Arch-Flamin, and Governour of* Cyprus.
Polydor, *Loves Inquisitor.*
Diophantes, *one of the Advocates of Loves Court.*
Palemon, { *A noble Cypriot in Love with* Bellinda, *and lov'd by* Filena.
Evander, { *A stranger come to Loves Kingdom on devotion.*
Pamphilus. { *A vicious young fellow, stranger to* Love's *Kingdom, and imagining all as vicious as himself.*
Philander, *a noble Cretian, &* Bellinda's *betroth'd*
Bellinda, { *a noble Cretian Nymph, stranger in* Love's *Kingdom.*
Filena, *a noble Cyprian Nymph.*
Amaranthe, *Governess of the Nymphs.*
Cloria, Mellissa, Lydia, *with others.* } *Nymphs of Cyprus.*
Chorus—*of Musicians, and young Virgins.*
2 Aruspices.
Love's Sacrificators.
The Popa, *or sacred Executioner.*
Guards, &c.
The Scene, Cyprus, *with all the Rules of Time and Place so exactly observ'd, as whilst for Time 'tis all compriz'd in as few hours as there are Acts; for Place, it never goes out of the view or prospect of Loves Temple.*

The Prologue.
Spoken by *Venus* from the Clouds.

IF ever you have heard of Venus *name*,
Goddess of Beauty, I that Venus *am*;
Who have to day descended from my sphere,
To welcome you unto Love's Kingdom *here*;
Or rather to my Sphere am come, since I
Am present no where more, nor in the Sky;
Nor any Island in the world, then this,
That wholly from the world divided is:
For Cupid; *you behold him here in me,*
(For there where Beauty *is,* Love *needs must be)*
Or you may yet more easily descry
Him 'mong the Ladies in each beauteous eye;
And 'mongst the Gallants, may as easily trace
Him to their bosoms, from each beauteous face.
May then fair Ladies you,
Finde all your Servants true;
And Gallants, may you finde
The Ladies all as kinde,
As by your noble favours you declare
How much you friends unto Love's Kingdom *are*
Of which your selves compose so great a part
In your fair Eyes, and in your loving heart.

Loves

Love's Kingdom.

Actus primus.

Enter Evander and Pamphilus.

The Scene, a delightful Landskip or Paisage.

Evander.

IS't not a pleasant place?
  Pamph. As e're I saw;
but I can see no Wenches yet, and that
I long for.

Ev. Why?

Pam. What a question's that? why do
the hungry long for meat I pray?

Ev. Then I
perceive you are an Epicure in Love,
and onely wo'd feed your body.

Pam. I am no Platonick Philosopher,
who while they feed their mindes,

do starve themselves; give me a Love that ha's some substance in it.

Ev. Well, this is no time
for to convert you; behold some coming here.

Enter a Troop of Nymphs and Shepherds, singing and dancing hand in hand.

The Song.

Come, and in this pleasant Grove,
Sacred to the Queen of Love,
Let our Voices and our Feet
In harmonious number meet;
Thus we sing the year throughout,
And merrily, merrily dance about. ⸃ *Exeunt.*

Ev. O happy Land! of all the sun surveys,
where thus perpetually they pass their dayes;
and if onely a living death it be,
or dying life to live in misery;
seeing their joyful lives, we well may say,
in all the world there are none live but they.

Pa. They're dainty wenches Ile say that for them,
and I must needs follow them.

Ev. Nay prethee.

Pam. Never talk of it, I can hold no more
then a good Greyhound when he sees the Hare,
or Hawk the Quarry; it is all my sport
and inclination, and by their mirth and Jollity
I know they're right, and of the Game.

Ev. There's your

errour

errour and ignorance now, who do not know;
how true vertue is a chearful thing,
rendring its favourites and followers far
more chearful too, more vertuous they are.

Pam. Hang Vertue! I know no chearfulness
but laughing, and I'me sure all the Nymphs here
are as supple and pliant as Kids-leather gloves,
a gentle pluck or two will easily draw them on.

Ev. How know you that? who came
but yesternight a stranger hither.

Pam. And how know you the contrary? who came
but hither yesternight along with me? let it suffice
I know all women by instinct; and
is not this *Love's Kingdom*? answer me to that.

Ev. Well, what then?

Pam. Why then I am in mine,
for I'me the loving'st creature
(thou doest not know me yet)
I tell thee I was such a forward Childe,
I fell in Love with my Nurse in the very Cradle,
and they were forc't to wean me,
for fear of spoiling her milk.

Ev. A great deflowrer of nurses it seems you are
but had you not better tarry till *Diophantes* comes,
who ha's promis'd to be our guide, and instruct us
in their manners and customs here?

Pam. Tarry you for him if
you please, my busines can best be dispatcht alone,
and I need no tutors nor conductors for't.

B 2

I thank you.

Ev. Well, thank your self if any harm come of it.

Pam. No harm I'le warrant you, but rather good, the good of posterity, whose business I am going about; and methinks I hear the Children yet unborn, crying out unto me to make haste, and so I will my little pretty sweet Babes. *Exit.*

Ev. what a wild fellow's this? I'm sorry & asham'd (now I know him better) that I came along with him to *Cyprus* here; who knows no more of Love then beasts do: and't so bravely impudent and vicious, he puts vice & impudence to the extreamest proof and shames not to be impudent enough: but here comes *Diophantes*. *Enter Diophantes.*

Dio. Noble *Evander*, I must demand your pardon if I instead of waiting on you, have made you wait for me; but I am Advocate in *Love's* Court you know, where so many petty quarrels of Lovers are daily to be reconcil'd. W'ave scarcely any vacancy at all, nor had we dispatcht so soon to day, but for the grand Solemnity i'th' Temple.

Ev. What's that I pray?

Dio. Why, 'tis the anniversary Feast of *Venus*, our Sea-born Goddesses first arrival here upon the *Cyprian* shore.

Ev.

Ev. And with good reason
you Celebrate that with all Solemnity,
that renders you so famous through all the world.

Di. And to add to th' general Solemnity oth' day
there's a particular Ceremony too
renders it more solemn.

Ev. What?

Dio. Why, you must know
that all strangers by th' Laws of *Cyprus* here
are after three moneths residence to swear
they love some one ith' Isle, or else be banisht;
now Sir, three moneths to day are just expir'd,
since there arriv'd a Nymph the most admir'd,
and most deserving admiration,
as ever in Love's Kingdom yet was known;
and whether she'l take the solemn Oath or no,
onely her self and the Deity do know;
for to all else 'tis doubtful.

Ev. Can it be doubted that any here sho'd love,
where they are all born and bred Lovers; the very
air inspires it, and 'tis as natural
for them to love, as 'tis to live and breath.

Dio. True Sir, but for our admiration
the gods work miracles sometimes, and she is one;
but where's your friend *Pamphilus*?

Ev. Rambled somewhere abroad,
I know not whither.

Dio. Of what humour, I pray,
and disposition is he.

B 3 *Ev.*

Ev. Why, harmless and merry, only a little wilde
Dio. He thinks perhaps our Nymphs are wanton here;
but Sir, I can assure you they are all
so chaste and pure, as Chrystal you wo'd say
is not more pure, nor Ice more clear then they:
And for the Land, know Sir, in all the spacious
world there's not a more religious place,
where Love with greater purity is profest,
nor serv'd and honour'd with more pious breast.
 Ev. I've understood so much, and therefore come
expresly hither on devotion,
to render my vows & off'rings at his sacred shrine
 Dio. I applaud you for't, and may the powers divine
for every prayer that you send up to them,
send you as many blessings down agen.
 Ev. Soft! who are those come here?
 Dio. Oh now you'l see
A noble Ceremony and Solemnity.

Enter Theotimus with Assistants of Loves Sacrificators, with Asperges and Thuribles besprinkling and incensing the place.

 The. Far hence be all profane, whilst here
With Solemn Rites thus every year,
To render all our Lovers true,
We element Love's Kingdom new;
That no heart may too strongly beat,
We give its fires a temperate heat;

We

Love's Kingdom.

We give its waters vertuous force,
To swage them (taken in their Source)
Fogs of perjur'd vows and oaths,
Which spotless truth and candour loaths,
We purge the Air from, and the Earth
From every strange and monstrous birth:
For as some Lands their monsters fear,
Lust onely is our monster here;
As others pois'nous beasts molest,
So avarice is our pois'nous beast:
From which when once a Land is freed,
Then, thên Love's Kingdom 'tis indeed. *(Exeunt*
  { *Manent Evander & Diophontes.*

Ev. A Ceremony as religious as great!

Di. Y'admire too soon, & have seen nothing yet,
if but compar'd to what you'l see anon,
worthy your sight and admiration.   *(Exeunt.*

Enter Palemon in desperate action, withheld by
  Polydor.

Pol. You wo'nt be mad?

Pal. I will be nothing but for Love,
and for Love I will be any thing;——
pray unhand me:—— Shall *Bellinda*, the
divine *Bellinda* be banisht hence to day,
and shall *Palemon* see it, and shall he live?

Pol. And shall the gallant and the brave
Palemon dye onely for fear of death?
how low——and poorly wo'd it shew!
and that's the worst; but I hope better still:

B 4   *Venus*

Venus the Goddess of this Isle
has oft done greater miracles then this,
to make one young and fair to love.

Pal. O *Polydor!* who has
miracles for hopes, has hopes too nigh despair.

Pol. I grant you,
but yours are far
from that ;—for ha's she not promis'd,
if any i'th' Isle she loves, it shall be you :
And is this no hope ? no comfort ?

Pal. Just as much
as 'mong the numerous and unhappy throng
of her excluded Lovers to stand next the door,
first expos'd to the affront, and nighest concern'd
in the disgrace.

Pol. Nay, if you give your self despair,
'tis in vain to give you hope ; suppose the worst :
If you love fair *Bellinda*, as you say,
and she perchance be banisht hence to day,
what hinders you from following her ? vainly and
ridiculously does he complain of Winter,
who by following the sun might still enjoy the
  Spring.

Pal. I,—but following an eclipsed Sun,
what shu'd he gain by it, but onely by
that fatal light to have every thing appear
more sad and dismal then if it absent were ?

Pol. Well, though it seem more to be wisht
  then hop'd,

that

that she shu'd love you ; yet take this from me,
your Nymphs are bashful, and so cautious too,
they will not seem to love, although they do :
and 'twod appear a miracle to me,
she shu'd not feel love who makes so many feel it;
or that her heart shu'd resist that alone,
was never yet resisted by any one : ——
But there's I fear some farther misery
in't, and the gods are highly offended w'ye,
or they'd ne're inflict on you as they do
so heavy a punishment to love one, who
neglects you ; and the while, to neglect one
so dearly loves ye, and see where she does come.
Enter Filena.

Fi. Where shu'd this Nymph be? she's not at home,
nor in the sacred Grove ; and 'tis too soon
to go to th' Temple yet.

Pol. Well, I'le leave you.

Pal. What, will you go
and leave me alone then ?

Pol. How can I leave you better accompanied?

Pal. In company of one I hate !

Pol. In company of one
who dearly loves you, and for your hate to her
in these pretty skirmishes, there is no fear
of danger ; for now y'are foes, and then
the peace is made, and you are friends agen,
and so I leave you. *Exit.*

Pal. What shall I do ? she has

spy'd

spy'd me, and there's no avoiding her ; I'de best
dissemble then, and by one importunity
avoid another: ——Gentle *Filena*, well met.

  Fi. Kinde looks   (*aside.*
that guild the sun-shine, as that guilds the day :
Kinde words,
whose ravishing sweetness melts into my heart
at sun-shine of those looks of his ; how I'me
o'rejoyed with them !

  Pal. I have a suit unto you.

  Fi. And I another to you.

  Pal. To me ! fye, fye,
Nymphs sue to men !

  Fi. Why, not *Palemon* here,
where Love's not onely Love, but Vertue too
it no wayes misbeseems a Nymph to wooe :——
But what's your suit ? you may be sure that I
  am too much yours *(Palemon)* to deny
you any thing.

  Pal. You know *Filena*, how much
I love *Bellinda*, and how much I long to know
if she loves me, which you can tell me best,
are confident of all the secrets of her breast.

  Fi. Some secrets she confides to me 'tis true,
but of her Love I know no more then you ;
for that's a warfare where each one's a spy,
and every rival is an enemy :   (know
She'd ne're trust me with't then , whom she does
an both a Lover, and her Rival too.

                                    Pal.

Pal. Howe're *Filena*, you do know at least
those softer minuts, when Nymphs minds are best
dispos'd for the impressions of Love;
in one of those then prethee do but move
my Suit unto her; especially before she goes
to th' Temple, when she must needs be more
dispos'd then ever, and thou shu'dst infinitely
oblige me by so dear a courtesie.
D'ye hear?

Fi. I do, and will you hear me now?

Pal. If y'ave any new thing to say I will,
but of old businesses I pray no more.

Fi. That can't be old that's every day renew'd.

Pal. And hów can that be new I pray,
that needs renovation every day?
But of this enough: — prethee *Filena* go,
and if you love me as you say you do; (shown,
know now's best time to shew't, for Love's best
by doing their wills we love before our own.

Fi. Well then, to shew
how much, how dearly I love you, I will go;
and though Love a burthen be,
which two hearts equally
shu'd bear, and then 'tis sweet and light:
But when once all the weight
lyes upon one alone,
a grievous and intollerable one:
my heart shall bear it yet, and ne're repine,
or else I'le not acknowledge it to be mine.

Pal.

Pal. That's bravely and nobly resolv'd.

Fi. But is there no hope, no pitty for *Filena*?

Pal. To deal ingeniously w'ye,
and not abuse you with civility,
There's pitty, but no hope; for *Bellinda* has all
my stock of Love, and consequently
for loving any other has rendred me so poor,
as I can dye, but I can love no more.

Fi. Since you are so resolv'd, *Palemon* know,
Filena too can dye as well as you;
and be assur'd that the same messenger
brings news *Palemon* does *Bellinda* wed,
shall carry back the news, *Filena*'s dead.

Pal. Soft, soft *Filena*, for I'de have you know,
to th' thing call'd dying there goes more then so;
and every Coward is valiant enough
to talk of death, but when it comes to th' proof,
their hearts do fail, as yours no doubt will too,
wherefore dear *Filena* I'le be gone,
and shall not fear to leave you here alone.
(spoken scornfully. Exit.

Fi. Cruel *Palemon*! is't not enough, that thou
refusest me, but thou must scorn me too?
This is not to be endur'd! one nobly born
can better suffer injury then scorn;
but what do I say wretch as I am, or how
com these high thoughts in one that's faln so low?
I'me now engag'd, what ever does befall,——
and those who are slaves to Love must suffer all.

Exit.   Enter

Love's Kingdom.

Enter Pamphilus, looking after her.

Pam. Hey! whurr! there boults another wench,
the Warren's all full of them,
and I, like a good Tumbler,
am ready to throw my self after every one: ——
and see here coms another!& alone too? ⎰ *Enter A-*
this opportunity is the shell that Love ⎱ *marantha.*
is hatched of, and the Nymphs here just like
young Lapwings run away with't on their heads;
you shall see how I'le accoast her now. ——
Fair Nymph, might I be so bold I pray,
to request the time o'th' day of you?

Am. Oh Sir, with all my heart,
it shall be any time oth' day you please for me,
I'le not stick w'ye for half an hour or so.

Pa. Lo ye there now! there's ne're a sextons wife
in all *Cyprus* co'd answer ye more courteously:
a kinde Wench I'le warrant her;——
Let's see what's next now?
Pox on't, I better know what to do with wenches
then what to say to them; and we Complementers
of the first head, when w'are past our legs & faces
are past the greatest part of our discourse:——
It shall be so, and how have you done I faith,
since I saw you last?

Am. Right and methodical!
how d'ye? and what's a clock? I'le wager now
next is, what news? or somewhat about the weather
the ordinary discourse of those who can

dis-

discourse of nothing,—and when was't I pray you saw me last?

Pam. Why, in *Plato's* great year, don't you remember it? I do as perfectly as if 'twere but to day; by the same token, meeting you just as I do now, I took you by the hand, and kissing it, led you just into such another Grove as this.

Am. Just no such matter; pray stay a little, sure you don't remember well.

Pam. Most perfectly, by the same token I saluted you too. *(She puts him by.*

Am. I knew you were quite wide, not me I'le assure you.

Pam. You can't deny't I'me sure.

Am. Indeed Sir but I can.

Pam. And thereupon I told you, that having so fair opportunity, but lose it, you'd never have the like agen.

Am. Opportunity for what?

Pam. Nay, if you know not that, we shal never have done;— com leave dissembling I know you Nymphs here are all so learned, as your husbands can teach you nothing on the marriage-night, but what you knew before.

Am. Bless me! I never heard man talk thus wildely!

Pam. And how first time you went abroad after fifteen, when you return'd agen,

you

Love's Kingdom. 15

you found y'ad left your gloves, handkercher, and maidenhead, with some such odd toyes behinde you.

Am. Wilder and wilder still! I begin to be afraid of him, pray let me go; is this discourse for Maids?

Pam. I, as good a Milkmaid as my Nurse I'le warrant you;—but stay, she may be one perhaps, and that 'tis makes her so shie and timerous, for maids apprehend the loss of a maidenhead as fearfully, as the loss of an arm or leg, and imagine they shall be maim'd for ever after.— Come, come, ne're fear, I perswade you to nothing but what I will do w'ye my self for company.

Am. I'me more and more afeard of him, I wo'd some body wo'd come to rid me of him, and see in happy time here's some, and yonder's more: now I may be   *{ Some pass over the*
as merry with him, *{ Stage.*
as he ha's been with me:—Cry mercy Sir, now I remember this *Plato's* great year you talk of as perfectly

Pam. Oh do you so! I knew you could not forget it.

Am. By the same token *Theotimus* chief Governour of the Isle past by with a numerous train just as we were alone together.

Pam. Yonder I think he comes indeed.

Am.

Am. When I made bold to ask you one questi-
Pam. What was that? (on Sir,
Am. Why, whether you lov'd dancing or no?
Ham. Oh exceedingly.

Am. Right, so you told me; and thereupon I said
he'd help you then to a certain spritely instrument
to dance after call'd a whip, a whip;
d'ye hear Sir, worth a hundred of
your Kits and Violins, to make such gallants as
your self to frisk and caper.

Pam. Umh! I remember nothing of all this now,
but beshrew me next *Plato*'s great year I fear
I shall indeed, 'less I get me gone the sooner.

Am. Nay, hark ye, hark ye Sir,
Pray don't go yet; now I remember me
I can tell ye what time o'th' day 'tis too.

Pam. As for that,
I know it now I thank you, it is time
for me to get me gone, as I take it. *(Exit.*
Am. Why then farewel my Platonick Philosopher,
and Anteplatonick Lover.

*Enter Theotimus, Chorus of Musicians, and young
Virgins, Polydor, Evander, Diophantes, Palemon, &c.*

The Song sung by a Bass, Tenor, and Treble.

Chorus sings. *Prais'd be the Deities above!*
  Ten. *We love.*
  Bass. *We lov'd.*
  Treb. *And we shall love.*

Cho.

Love's Kingdom.

Cho. O ye blest immortal Powers!
Grant this happy Land of ours
  1. Pure fires,
  2. Pure fewel,
  Cho. All things pure,
And that our flames may ever dure.

  The. Now Children, in a word to tell,
what noble Love is, (mark me well)
it is the counterpoise that mindes
to fair and vertuous things inclines;
it is the gust we have, and sence,
of every noble excellence;
it is the pulse, by which we know
whether our souls have life or no;
and such a soft and gentle fire,
as kindles and inflames desire,
until it all like Incense burns,
and unto melting sweetness turns.

  Ev. Whose heart
melts not within his breast at hearing this?

  The. Who's that?

  Dio. A noble stranger come hither on
devotion unto Love's sacred Shrine.

  The. He's welcome.   (*Evan. kisses his hands*

  Pal. Somewhat more then this to boo't,
by experience I can adde unto't;
Love is a union of all
we happy and unhappy call;
a mixture where together meet

C   both

You I dare trust with secrets, which I ne're
durst trust with any since my coming here:
I love,——but Oh! if any list'ning ear
shu'd have o'reheard me now, as 'tis my fear!
And see where this inquisitive Nymph do's come?
Wo'd she were deaf, or else that I'de been dumb.

  Fi. Ifaith, Ifaith.   (*Enter Filena.*
I'me glad I've found you.

  Bell. Why?

  Fi. For now 'tis clear you love.

  Bell. How so? —'tis as I fear'd,
she has o'reheard me.   (*Aside.*

  Fi. These very trees and woods declare it.

  Bel. Ay me! this 'tis to trust ones minde (*aside.*
with trees, whose leaves whisper with every wind,
with woods, whose very walks & shades have ears,
and babbling Eccho that tells all it hears.

Fi. She fears, 'tis a good sign, Ile urge her further—
your solitude and retirement too confirms it;
for no Nymph here
retir'd from company ever walks alone;
but Love is still gentle companion of
her solitary thoughts.

  Bell. If that be all, 'tis well.   (*Aside.*

Fi. And why shu'd you with so much caution now
conceal this from me? as I did not know
how Love d d all things out of chaos make,
and all to s' s wo'd agen turn back:
If all this did not love, from Gods and men

to senseless and inanimate things agen;
and what a monster shu'd *Bellinda* prove,
if onely she of all things did not love? (tongue,

Bel. Of all the Nymphs that ever spoke with
this Nymph has Magick I must bless me from!

Fi. Where is the friendship y've so long profest
to make me such a stranger to your breast?

Bel. Trust me dear friend, if what you say be true,
I am more stranger to my breast then you.

Fi. See how you blush now when you tell me so!

Bel. Ay me! mine own blushes betray me too!
What is it can be secret in a Lover,
when even their blushes do their Loves discover?

Fi. What and sigh too! nay then you love, 'tis clear;
for, but for Love, none ever sighed here.

Bel. my sighs betray me too! how many traytors
have Lovers about them? *(Aside.*

Fi. But why shu'd you sigh! you live happily,
and sighs are for the miserable, such as I:———
Palemon loves you, and so loves you too,
as he even pines away for Love of you;
consumes with grief, languishes with despair,
melts into tears, and sighs himself to air;
faith, give him some comfort e're you go
unto the Temple, sweet *Bellinda* do;
poor Youth, he's in so desperate estate,
I fear, lest after it may come too late.

Bel. What greater comfort can he expect of me,
then that, if any i'th' Isle I love, 'tis he?

C 3 *Fi.*

Fi. Poor comfort, that it shall be him alone,
if any i'th' Isle you love, if you love none;
this is to mock his hopes; and they deny
rather then grant, who promise doubtfully.

Bell. More (*Filena*) I neither will nor can
give him, until I go to th' Temple anon,
and there consult the Gods what I shu'd do.

Fi. Consult your own thoughts rather,
and your minde.

Bell. 'Tis not easie as you think to finde
the source and origin of our thoughts and minde;
of which t'one is so deep, t'other so high,
as there are Opticks made to pierce the sky,
plummets to sound the bottom o'th' ocean;
but for to pierce and sound a heart there's none.

Within. *Bellinda, Bellinda.*

Bell. Here! who calls? *(Enter Polydor.*

Pol. 'Tis I.

Fi. Gentle *Polydor*,
what news from th' Temple w'ye?

Pol. Nothing, but onely all's prepared there
for th' grand solemnity, and onely fair
Bellinda's presence expected.

Bell. If't be so,
let us away.

Pol. Soft, 'tis not time to go this hour yet.

Bell. And that a day will seem to be
a moneth, a year, a very age to me. (*Exit joyfully.*

Pol. D'ye think she loves?

Fi.

Fi. I know not, let's divine,
and joyn your observations to mine:——
D'ye mark with how great joy away she went?
none goes so chearfully to banishment.

Pol. But if her body's here, and mind elsewhere,
'tis she does banish us, and not we her.

Fi. Well, if she love, I wonder at her art
can carry fire so smother'd in her heart,
as none nor by the flame nor smoak can know
whether sh'ave any in her breast or no.

Pol. And if she do not love agen, then she
of all the Nymphs I yet did ever see,
the most my admiration does move,
t have so much beauty, and so little love.

Fi. I'le follow and observe her better.

Pol. Do,
and I'le but stay awhile and follow you.

     (*Exit Filena. Enter Pamphilus*

Pam. That Wench!
that wench wo'd I give a limb for now,
though I halted to an Hospital for it, (and there
are many have ventur'd as far for wenches as that
comes to) I must needs have her, and he here
shall be my Agent in the business.——
D'ye hear, d'ye hear Sir, a word with you I pray.

Pol. With me! your pleasure Sir?

Pam. D'ye know that Nymph there?

Pol. Very well, what then?

Pam. Why then I shu'd desire

your

your better acquaintance;
for look ye, suppose a man
shu'd have a minde unto her.

Pol. A minde, what minde?

Pam. Why, a moneths minde or so.

Pol. Why then, after a moneth you may be rid of't.

Pam. I hope Sir you do not mock me?

Pol. Indeed Sir, but I do,——
you must pardon me.

Pam. 'Tis well you confess it, and ask my pardon,
I shu'd be very angry else, I can tell you

Pol. This is some simple stranger, ignorant of
our manners and customs, rather meriting
pitty then anger. *(Aside.*

Pam. He understands nothing but plain *(aside.*
down-right language I see, that calls every thing
by its right name:—Well Sir, since I perceive
you are a little dull, in plainer terms
I'de fain—— you understood me. *(Whispers.*

Pol. How Sir!

Pam. Even so Sir,

Pol. D'ye know where you are?

Pam. Why, in *Love's Kingdom*, where shu'd I be?

Pol. But not
in *Lust* - remember that.

Pam. Pox a these nice
distinctions! that onely serve to break
Dunces heads, and keep Maidenheads so long,
till they are quite marr'd:—— Come, come, I know

no

no other love but what I've told you.

Pol. Then you must be taught,
and learn other language too, or else this Isle
(I can tell you) will prove too hot for you.

Pam. Wo'd the Nymphs were not so cold,
and let the Isle be what it will. (*Aside.*

Pol. And now to instruct you a little better, know
that for all lewd and lascivious speeches we
have a gentle punishment here, called whipping.

Pam. Gentle d'ye call it?

Pol. And for fowl libidinousness,
an other excellent remedy call'd castrating
that takes it clear away.

Pam. Clear with a witness,
bless me and all mine from it:
why this is cruel sir——
have you no regard then to peoples infirmities?

Pol. O yes, a special one, for your wild and unruly
heats of youth, w'ave an admirable way
of cooling 'um, by marrying 'um unto
old women of fourscore, there's a cooler for you.

Pam. A cooler with a vengeance! ah ha!
it makes my teeth chatter in my head to think of it
but sure sir y'are not in earnest all this while?

Pol. It seems sir you love to jest, but look to't, and
say y'ad fair warning; —and so farewel. (*Exit.*

Pam. Farewel quoth ye?
marry 'tis time to bid farewel indeed
if this be so, whipping, castrating, and

mar-

marrying to old women of fourscore !
a great consolation for a man that loves
a wench ; but he said all this sure
onely to fright me ;
yet let him say what he will,
woo'd I had that wench say I.

Enter Amaranthe, Cloria, Lydia, Melissa, &c.

Whow? here comes a whole ocean of them!
now am I in my element, and I shall wallow
like a Porposs amongst them.

Am. What my Platonick Philosopher,
and Anteplatonick Lover agen?

Pam. 'Slid is she there? I'd best be gon then,
as feard of her as a dog is of a whip.

Am. What is he going? I must needs have
some sport with him before he goes.——
Hark ye, hark ye sir, pray stay a little.

Pam. Now will she trappan me
into a whipping, I'm sure;
yet I am such a fool I must needs tarry.

Am. These nymphs here wo'd be glad
of your better acquaintance:

Pam. With all my heart.

Lyd. What means *Amarinthe*?

Am. Come nearer, nearer yet; now nymphs
look on him (I pray) and mark him well.

Pam. This goes well hitherto——
I must prepare my self to court um now.

Am. And

Am. And now be't known unto you all,
he's one whom y'are to bless your selves from, as
from some ghost or goblin.——

Pam. How's this?

Am. For he'l haunt you,
haunt you worse then they,
and stick t'ye faster then burrs, or rather pitch
that defiles all it touches: there is no
purifying your selvs a month after h'as once been
in your company.

Mel. Bless us from him!

Pam. The devil's in her:
in what a fair way of courtship was I, and how
sh'as put me out of it?

Am. Yet (wo'd ye think it?)
he imagins all the nymphs are in love with him,
nay will swear it, if they look but on him once,
and then talk so lewdly, as shews him all
groom and foot-boy within,
however without he appears a Gentleman.

Pam: She'l make me all groom
and foot-boy presently, she'as half
transformed me already.

Am. Nay, hold up your head sir,
and ben't asham'd of your commendations.

Pam. Commendations d'ye call it? I wonder what
are your reproaches, if these be your commendations.   (*Aside.*

Lyd. Sure *Amaranthe* you wrong him.

Pam. I

Pam. I indeed,
does she sweet heart,

Lyd. Forbear, and know your distance Sir.

Am. Nay he's like
a Spannel, hold him at arms end, or he'l
be in your bosom presently.

Mel. Nay, now y'are too cruel.

Am. If he wo'd either spare
his own or others modesty, I wo'd be
content to spare him yet?

Pam. I must suffer I see.

Am. But see *Theotimus* coming,——cultivating
our youth, and sowing in their tender mindes
the seeds of all our future happiness, for
'tis not the culter o'th' Land, but of the minde
makes people happy;
and as that's done well or ill,
so they are happy or unhappy still.

Enter Theotimus, *Chorus of Musicians, and young
Virgins,* Diophantes, Evander, *&c.*

The. Now tender Virgins all draw near,
And Loves diviner doctrine hear;
First, Nymphs be modest as you go,
For just as by the pulse we know
The bodies state, so we as well
By th' eyes, the state o'th' minde may tell
And rowling eyes do but betray
A heart that rowls as well as they.

Chor.

Chor. sings. *O fly then far*
Glances that are
But outward signs, by which we finde
The inward temper of the minde;
And rowling eyes do but betray
A heart that rowls as well as they.

Pam. Hei day, now will these wenches wear their eyes like spectacles on their noses, and look as demurely as Cows in bon-graces.

The. Then for your kisses, oh, be sure
No Virgins ever those endure;
For you are flowers and blooming Trees,
And men are such deflowring Bees:
Let once their kisses light upon ye,
They soon will suck all sweetness from ye,
And womens lips with kissing us'd
Will look but just like Cherries bruis'd.

Chor. sings. *O fly then far*
Kisses that are
Like Bees that suck all sweetness from (ye;
Let 'um once but light upon you:
And womens lips with kissing us'd,
Will look but just like Cherries bruis'd.

Pam. Now will these wenches lips grow as cold as dogs noses, if they leave off kissing once.

The. But above all take heed agen
You fly and shun the touch of men;
For there's no canker more devours,
Nor mildew more blasts tender flowers,

Then

Then men will you, whose lightest touch
Will soon your fresher beauties smutch;
And once but tainted in your hue,
You well may bid the world adieu.

  Chor. sings. *O fly then far*
            Touches that are
            So blasting, as the lightest touch
            Will soon your fresher beauties smutch;
            And once but tainted in your hue,
            You well may bid the world adieu.

  Pam. 'Tis time to bid the world adieu indeed, if there be no touching 'um.

  Th. Now that we ben't expected there, 'tis time to th' Temple to repair: ——— set forwards there before.   (*Exeunt.*

  Manent Diophantes, Evander, Pamphilus, Amaranthe, Cloria, Lydia, Melissa.

  Ev. Oh! *Pamphilus* well met; and how d'ye finde the nymphs here, ha?

  Pam. As I co'd wish, the kindest lovingst souls as e're I met withal.

  Am. How's this! let's stand close, and over hear him.

  Pam. You need not multiply the Phenix to sum up the number of all the maidenheads I shall leave in *Cyprus* here, before I've done with 'um

  Am. D'ye hear?

  Ev. Is't possible

  Pam. No, no, I knew not the humor

                          and

Love's Kingdom. 31

and disposition of the nymps here, I.
Em. Troth, and so I think still.   (*Aside.*
Pam. I hope now you'l believe me another time?
Ev. It may be so, but now I swear I do not. (*Aside.*
Dio. Yet let us sooth and humour him to have
some sport with him;——
you know all the Nimphs here then?
Pam. O most intimately.
Diop. Amaranthe, Cloria, Lydia, Melissa?
Pam. All, all——
and have had favours from every one of them,
this Ring from one, this Ribband from a second,
this Jewel from a third.
Mel. What a lying fellow's this!
Dio. And what think you of *Cloria*?
Pam. She kisses well,
I've gone no farther with her yet, but there
is hope I may in time.
Clo. Shall I indure this?
Am. Nay prethee,
Dio. And *Lydia*?
Pam. With her I must confess
I've had a little more familiarity.
Lyd. There's no induring this!
Am. Yet this was he
you thought I wrong'd.
Lyd. Hang him, none can, but onely
by reporting too well of him.
Pam. For *Amarinthe* she's the coyest of 'um all,
Am. I

Am. I thank you.

Pam. And was so angry with me for
a kiss I stole from her, but I soon pacified her:

Dio. As how?

Pam. Why, I told her that rather
then that shud make a war betwixt us,
which was wont to be the signe of peace with others,
I'd make her double satisfaction;
and for one kiss I took from her, wo'd give
her two.

Ev. So then (as you imagin'd 'um) you finde
all the Nymphs here as supple and plyant as
kids leather Gloves, a gentle pluck or two
will easily draw 'um on.

Pam. Draw 'um on! wou'd some body wou'd
draw 'um off for me:
I fear I shall be ravisht by 'um.

Am. Out upon him, I'le hear no more,
let's go, and as we pass, shew him all
the neglect and scorn we can possible.

They pass by him frowningly and Exeunt.

Dio. D'ye mark how they frown upon him?

Pam. Favours, meer favours, believe it Gentlemen,
and onely invitations to follow 'um;
you see how I am courted, and must pardon me.

Exit.

Dio. The man's as impudent as vain I see,
and though this hitherto be but in jest

you

Love's Kingdom.

you whom he counts his friend may tell him beſt,
If he imagines with injurious lyes
To get him honour by their injuries:
Our Nymphs are all of ſuch unqueſtion'd Fame,
He'l ſooner puniſhment, then credit gain. (*Exeunt.*
         Enter Palemon.

Pal. This way the fair *Bellinda* is to paſs
Unto the Temple, and although ſhe has
Forbid me ſpeaking to her on pain of her
Diſpleaſure, I may ſee her howſoe're;
And as ſhe goes to th' Temple, feaſt mine eyes,
Which happineſs ſhe to my tongue denyes. ——
     Enter Bellinda, Filena, Polydor.
See where ſhe comes, and now it fares with me
As with thoſe ſick, who whilſt they long to ſee
The cup they may not taſte, become but more
Thirſty with ſight of't then they were before.

Fi. Behold *Palemon*, as I've appointed him
ith way, can we invent no ſtratagem
to make her now with favourable eye
regard him? think, I'le ſecond you.

Pol. I'le try:
whoſe that *Palemon*?

Fi. Think it be,
but let's go on and think not on him.
             Exeunt Bellinda and Polydor.

Pal. She my enemy!

Pol. Ben't deceiv'd *Palemon*, for
'twas ſaid to make her think of you the more.

All. Oh hear our vows and prayers as we
do purely love and honour thee.   *(Soft Musick.*
   Fi. Thou doest confirm us by this Harmony,
O Love our Vows are pleasing unto thee.
   Ev. Now I perceive it is our faults, not theirs,
If when we pray, the gods don't hear our prayers.
   Dio. Peace now, the other Ceremony begins.
   Fi. Let us retire then, and give place to them.

Enter Theotimus, Chorus of Musicians one way, Bellinda the other, brought in by Polydor, Pamphilus, &c.

Chorus sings.

Divinest Love does all command,
In fire and water, air and land;
And all with his commands inspire
In land and water, air and fire.

   The. Where is the Nymph?
   Pol. Great Sir, behold her here;——
bear back, bear back, room for the Nymph there.
   Pam. Now will he break my head,
onely to shew his authority, (you'l see)
'less I get me out of the way the sooner.
   The. Then fair and gentle Nymph draw near,
And all our Ceremonies hear,
Which to Religion do dispence
Both Mystery and Reverence:
We first must charm you silent, then
Must vail and blinde your eyes agen;

That

Love's Kingdom.

That you may see and speak with none,
Untill the Ceremony's done:
Then y'are to go to th' sacred Cell,
Where a full hour you are to dwell,
Before you are produc't to swear.
You love some one in *Cyprus* here;
Or else (refusing it) be sent
Into perpetual banishment.——
If then y'ave any thing to say,
Now speak it freely whilst you may.

  Bel. Prudence assist me, thou that best canst tell,
                                                    (Aside.
What I shu'd say, and what I shu'd conceal;——
Knowing great sir, how w'ar the gods chief care,
More dear to them, then to our selves we are:
Behold *Bellinda* here resigned stands
To obey your Laws, and their divine commands.

  The. A wise and pious Resignation!
Most pleasing unto Heaven, and such an one
As even necessitates the Gods to grant
All that we mortals crave, and all we want.——
Reach us the sacred Wand
to charm her silent then.

The Charm.

Still-born Silence, thou that art
Flood-gate of the deeper heart,
Off-spring of a heavenly kinde,
Frost o'th' mouth, and thaw o'th' minde;

D 3   *Admi-*

Pam. This is worse then to'ther!
Did you but know how much I love you,
you'd never refuse my courtesie.

2 And did you but know how little I care for it,
you'd never offer it.

Ham. Hei ho! have ye the heart to hear me
sigh thus, and never pitty me?

2 Yes indeed, and to laugh at you for it too,
to hear you sigh thus
like a broken-winded bellows,
or a dry pump and spend so much breath in vain,
as we shall never wonder hereafter
at *Lapland* Witches selling winde so cheap.

Pam. But I shall alwayes wonder,
that here in *Venus* School the Nymphs shu'd learn
no more compassion.

2 Now ye talk of Schools,
I must to the Graces Grove,
where all the Nymphs are gone
to learn their lessons. *(Exit.*

Pam. And I will follow them;
strange that all shu'd be honest!
I have heard of one or two in a Countrey, or so,
but all, all, was never heard of before.
I don't despair yet.
Well. *(Exit.*

Enter

Love's Kingdom.

Enter Amaranthe, Filena, Cloria, Lydia, Meliſſa.

The Scene, the Graces Grove, the Statues of the three Graces in the midſt, all hand in hand embrac'd.

Am. Now Nymphs, here in the Graces Grove,
A place which Beauty moſt does love,
And gentle Love moſt highly prize,
Let's fall unto our exerciſe
Of ſtudying all thoſe gracious parts,
Which moſt do take and conquer hearts.
{ *Enter Pamphilus.*

Pam. Now will I ſtand here conceal'd,
and obſerve them; they ſay, all women when
they are alone, put off their modeſties;
I ſhu'd be glad to ſee it.

Am. Firſt Nymphs, in honour of the Graces
Let us compoſe our looks and faces
To gentle ſmiles, for no frowns here
In any face ſhu'd e're appear.

Pam. If I thought they would not frown,
I ſhu'd ſoon be amongſt them.

Am. And next, as we our faces do,
We muſt compoſe our garments too
With ſuch a decency, as beſt
Becomes the modeſt to be dreſt.

Pam. Wo'd they'd put off their garments once,
that's it I look for.

Am.

Am. But since the graces of the minde
Are those which most adorn our kinde,
It ought to be our chiefest care
To render our interiours fair;
Counting th' exterior nothing else,
But outward garments of our selves,
　Pam. Give me the out-side,
and take the inside who's list.
　Am. Other Graces there are beside,
Which Nymphs shu'd carefully provide,
As dancing, singing, and such arts,
Which through the Sences strike their hearts;
And give (where ever they are found)
That dangerous yet gentle wound,
Which never can be cur'd again,
Till *Hymen* ease their amorous pain.
　Pam. I co'd ease and cure it a great deal better,
if they would but let me alone with them.
　Am. Then let us sing, that Eccho may
The sound unto the Woods conveigh;
And after raising it more high,
The Woods conveigh it to the Sky;
That heaven and earth may both partake
The Harmony your Voices make.
　　　　　　　(*Here the Nymphs sing.*
　Pam. I co'd make othergess musick with them,
if I were but master of the Quire amongst them.
　Am. Now let's have a dance, to shew,
How that which does enchant men so,

Is

Is not the Magick of the face,
The red and white, nor bodies grace;
But 'tis the Magick of the feet,
Where all harmonious numbers meet.
(Here the Nymphs dance.

Pam. I think there's witchcraft in't indeed,
for I can as well be hang'd as hold now,
but I must have a frisk amongst them;
Hei for our Town! *(He comes out dancing.*

Fi. A man amongst us!
what insolence is this? *(Exit.*

Pam. Nay, never look so strange on it,——
there are those can dance too, you
shall see else. *}he dances 'em about one after another.*
Mel. Was ever seen the like?
Pam. Yes twenty times,——How say you?
Lyd. Away, are you not asham'd?
Pa. No indeed, I was never asham'd in my life—
nay, you must have your turn too.
Clo. Let me go,—or I'le cry out else.
Pam. 'Tis yet too soon,
I'le give you more cause presently.
Lyd. Away *Melissa.* *(Exit.*
Mel. Away *Cloria.* *(Exit.*
Clo. Away *Lydia.* *(Exit.*
Am. Away all of you,
this is a rudeness must be complained of.
(Exeunt omnes, manet Pamphilus.
Pam. Look ye! is not this a lamentable case?
that

that all the Nymphs fhu'd flye me as chickens do
a Kite, or birds fome ftrange Owl; yet I proteft,
I mean them no more harm, then their fathers did
their mothers, as they fhu'd foon perceive, if they
wo'd but try me once; I fear I fhall never do
any good on them, yet I muft follow them ftill:
For the devil's in't, when once we begin
to follow wenches, we can never give over. *Exit*

Enter Philander folus.

*The Scene, the Cyprian Shore, a waving Sea afar
off difcovered, &c.*

Phi. Hail happy Ifland! Natures chiefeft care,
Where all things love, and all things fruitful are;
Where Spring-tide makes perpetual Refidence,
And rigid Winter's ever banifht hence;
In you, (O bleft and happy Land) in you
I fhall finde her, (if the Oracle be true)
Through all the Iflands of th' *Egean* Main,
Thefe three moneths I have fought, and fought in
Till here arriving now at laft, I fee   (vain;
So vafte a folitude, as amazes me!
Nor on the barren Mauritanean Shore,
Or *Lybian* Defart, fcarcely co'd be more!
                         (*Enter Palemon.*

Pal. I'le hide me no longer from my fears, nor fly
The danger, 'tis childifh and cowardly,
And (well confidered) rather does increafe
Our dangers and our fears, then make them lefs;
                              For

For looking through that false optick fear,
Danger does still more terrible appear,
And terrors in the dark far more afright
(Th' imagination of't) then in the light:
I'le then to the Temple, and whate're befal
By help of this, I am prepar'd for all.
> *Pointing to his Sword.*

Phi. Sir, might a stranger here desire to know
Why all your houses are deserted so,
As if some plague had swept 'um; and the **Land**
Depopulated, as if some enemies hand
Had mow'd it with the sword! to me it does
Appear to wonder strange, that love shu'd **thus**
Leave his own Land unpeopled, whilst he
Peoples all others so abundantly!

Pal. Know Sir, 'tis not for want of people here
Loves Kingdom does so desolate appear,
But just as we perceive from every part,
The blood does all retire unto the heart,
In any great commotion or dismay;
So all the people, in no less, to day
Are gone to th' Temple, in expectancy
O'th' issue of our great solemnity.

Phi. What's that?

Pal. Why, by the Laws of *Cyprus*, here
All strangers after three moneths are to swear
They love some one i'th Island, or be sent
Away into perpetual banishment:
Now Sir, this oath a Nymph to day must take,

Phi. And

Phi. And why shu'd that
so great commotion make?
  Pal. 'Cause she's the joy or grief of every one;
Joy if she stay, and grief if she be gone.
  Phi. What is this Nymph so much exacts your care,
  Pal. One who some three moneths since arrived here,
Wrack't on the Coast; (the rest all drown'd but she)
In whom appear'd so great divinity;
It was another *Venus* you'd have swore;
Born of the Sea, and landing on the shore.
  Phi. Just so long 'tis since she was stoln away
from *Crete*, to barbarous pyrates made a prey;
and her name, Sir,
  Pal. Bellinda, Sir, they call
this admirable Nymph:
  Phi. Her name and all?
and where is she?
  Pal. I'th sacred Cell inclos'd,
ready to take the oath.
  Phi. And is't suppos'd
she'l take it?
  Pal. That as yet, there's none can tell
But this (unto my grief) I can full well,
That less she does, you here behold in me
The wretchedst Lover ever eye did see,
Or ever liv'd in memory of men
                      Phi. Hea-

Phi. Heavens! what do I hear? —are you
  her Lover then?

Pal. Shu'd I deny it, these Trees wou'd tell
  you I am,
Upon whose Barks so oft I've carv'd her name;
This shore so oft my lamentations hears —
And Sea that I've augmented with my tears;
As with my sighs the air; these Sir, all these
Will tell you I am, though I shu'd hold my peace.

Phi. O Heaven! in vain why did you valor give,
If I can hear this now, and let him live?
But stay, if seeing and loving her be a crime,
I must kill all mankinde as well as him;
For all wo'd guilty be, and you shou'd finde
None innocent, but the senseless, and the blinde:
I'le then suspend my anger, till I know
Whether *Bellinda* does love him or no;
For there, there onely the offence does lie,
Else he's the person offended, and not I;
For never Tyrant invented greater pain,
Then 'tis to love, and not be lov'd again.—
It shall be so —and pray Sir, mayn't one see
This Nymph you speak of?

Pal. Please you go with me
Unto the Temple Sir, there you may both
See her, and hear her take the sacred Oath.

Phi. So confident!

Pal. I've a promise Sir from her
makes me hope so.

Phi. Then

Phi. Then I may well despair—— (*Aside.*
yet will I not be jealous, for that,
Though it begins in love, does end in hate,
And I her love to mine so far prefer,
As I may hate my self, but never her——
Yet it is strange, if what he sayes be true!

Pal. But has she any relation unto you,
you seem so much concern'd for her, Sir?

Phi. No other
But what a Sister has unto a Brother;
If she be th' same as I imagine her:

Pal. Then I beseech you Sir,
till some more near
relation and bond may binde me t'ye,
you wo'd be pleas'd for to accept of me
for your most humble Servant.

Phi. That Sir, I
may not; but please you do me the courtesie
to shew me th' way unto the Temple, and you
shou'd much oblige me.

Pal. That Sir I shall do } *Exit*
to shew my obedience, or any thing I may. } *Pal.*

Phi. I'le follow you then,
please you to lead the way.——
Now dearest Love, in this thy kingdom be
As kinde and as propitious unto me.
As through thy grace and favour I hope to finde
Ease for my wearied limbs and troubled minde;
And

Love's Kingdom.

And a calm port and sure retreat at last
After so many storms and dangers past. (*Ex. Phil.*
Finis Actus tertii.

ACTUS 4.

Enter Palemon and Philander.

*The Scene, Loves Temple, as before, two Aruspices
with burning Censors, &c.*

Palemon.

Now hêre Love at thy sacred shine
I offer up these vows of mine,———
Father of dear and tender thoughts,
Thou who the hardest bosom softs;
Soften *Bellinda's* heart, and make
Her but thy dear impressions take;
So shall I burn Arabian Gums,
And offer up whole Hecatombs
Upon thy Altar, whilst thy fires
Shall shine as bright as my desires.

1. *Arus.* Whilst he the Deity does invoke
The flame ascends in troubled smoke:

Phi. What sort of offering mine shall be,
Divinest Love's best known to thee;
Nor spices, nor Arabian Gums,
Nor yet of beasts whole Hecatombs:

H

These

These are too low and earthly, mine
Are far more heavenly and divine,
An Adamantine faith, and such
As jealousie can never touch:
A constant heart, and loyal breast,
These are the offerings thou lov'st best.

   2. *Arus.* Loves fires ne're brighter yet appear'd,
Who e're thou art, thy vows are heard.

Enter Theotimus, *Chorus of Musicians one way,* Bellinda *'tother, with all the Nymphs,* Polydor, Evander, Diophantes, Pamphilus, *&c.*

   Pal. Now see here where she comes.
   Phi. Her noble frame,
habit, and stature tells me 'tis the same?
   The. Why comes she not away?
   Pol. What ails she there?
   Am. Help, help, she swounds:
   Lyd. Give her, give her more air?
   The. Hold, hold, I charge you, and let none presume to touch the consecrated veil.
   Pol. Behold she's come
to her self again;
   The. Let the Solemnity
go on then.
   Phi. Now I clearly see 'tis she.
   The. Now on this Book here lay your hands,
Cover'd with skins of Doves and Swans,
And *Love* so help you as you swear,
Unfeignedly you love one here.

Phi. Now

Love's Kingdom. 51

Phi. Now *Philander* thou shalt know
whether she be true or no:
Pal. And I know my destiny,
Whether I'me to live or dye.
The. Thus I uncharm your tongue, now speak
And to our joyes your silence break.
Bel. Then by Loves sacred deity I swear,
I love one in the Isle.
Phi. What do I hear!
The. Enough,——the charm agen, I thus apply:
Pal. O me, most happy!
Phi. And most unhappy I!
The. Now bear her to the Cell again,
Where yet an hour she's to remain;
Suffer'd to see nor speak with none
Untill the hour be past and gone.

Chor. sings.

Praised be Love does all command
In fire and water, air, and land,
And all with his commands inspire
In land and water, air and fire. (*Exeunt:*
Manet Filena.

Fi. Bellinda Love! nay then my fears I see
Were not in vain, and nothing's left for me,
But onely death; when nothing else prevails,
That's the last remedy, and never fails.
  ℥ *Enter Palemon, and seeing her, returns.*
Stay, stay *Palemon*,

E 2   This

This is the laſt time we ſhall ever meet;
Stay then and hear me, it is nobler yet
To kill me like the baſilisk with your ſight,
Then like the Parthians, kill me with your flight.—
But he is gone (alas) and does deny
Me the laſt office of humanity
Of cloſing of my dying eyes in death,
And when I expire, receive my lateſt breath.—
The many wayes that lead to death do make
Me yet irreſolute which way to take;
But ſome way I muſt take, and ſpeedily
Reſolve upon it too, what e're it be. *{Exit.*

Enter Pamphilus.
The Scene, The precints of the Temple.

Pam. Strange! that I can finde no way to faſten on theſe Nymphs? here comes one now, and I'le try a way with her that ſeldom fails they ſay.—— { *Enter firſt Nymph.* } Fair Nymph pleaſe you to accept theſe Jewels here?

1. Nym. Wherefore Sir?

Pam. Onely to buy your love, nothing elſe

1. Nym. Bleſs me! Simony in love! { *Throws them away and exit.* }

Pam. This is the firſt wench as ever I met withal, that refus'd preſents when they were offer'd her, and I think will be the laſt.——

This

Love's Kingdom. 53

This is a ſtrange Countrey,
where a man can't get a wench
neither for love nor money? well, I perceive
this handling 'um with ſo much ceremony
is that which ſpoils 'um,
and makes 'um ſo nice and ticklish
there is no touching 'um:
women ſhu'd be handled like nettles,
but preſs them hard
and you may do any thing with them,
and I'le try that way with the next I meet.

Enter Filena.

Fil. I have bethought me of a way to dye
and muſt go ſeek out *Amaranthe's* help.

Pam. Stay Lady, a word with you I pray
before you go.   (*Layes hold on her,*

Fil. Was ever ſuch a rudeneſs? unhand me ſir,
and know that Virgins are like ſacred Reliques
beheld with reverence; but let men come
to touch 'um once, their reverence is gone,——
what wou'd you with me?

Pam. What a queſtion's that?
when a man's alone with a woman, you
may eaſily gueſs what he wou'd have with her.

Fil. Hence and avoid my ſight, for now I ſee,
How all that we call vicious is in thee;
Foul corrupter of honour, as cankers of faireſt
 flowers,
Shame of thy Sex, diſhonourer of ours!

E 3   *Pam.* Whow,

Pam. Whow, whow ! is the woman mad ?

Fi. Avoid my sight I say, thy glowing eyes like Basilisks will kill me else ; go and repent thee of thy crying sins.   (*Exit.*

Pam. What are those ?
I know no crying sins I have,
but mine own Bastards:——Well, go thy wayes, if e're thou marriest, I'le give thy husband this comfort, he shall have no other issue of thee but nails and teeth, if thou be'st such a Vixen.
    (*Enter Evander and Diophantes.*

Ev. Now *Pamphilus*, what's the matter, that the Nymph is gone in such a rage away ?

Pam. Nothing, nothing, onely I offer'd her the courtesie oth' Countrey, and she refus'd it, that is all.

Ev. Why then, I see you need not multiply the Phenix, to sum up all the Maidenheads you'l leave in *Cyprus*,
before you have done with them.

Pam. Well, well, you do not know yet.

Ev. Yes, but we do Sir, more then you imagine—
of a certain Nymph, you met in *Plato*'s great year, and how she entertain'd you.

Pam. 'Slid ! how comes he to know of that ?

Ev. And of divers other encounters with them since, when you could not desire to be better mockt and laught at then you were.

Dio. And now Sir, pray

as you finde our Nymphs here, so report of them;
and know 'tis not the way
for men to gain them reputation here,
to make themselves more vicious then they are.

Pam. Nay, if he chide once I'me gone.

Ev. Y'are deceiv'd, he chides you not,
but rather gives you good counsel.

Pam. That is as 'tis taken,——'tis good councel
to those who mean to follow it;——
but to me 'tis flat chiding,
and I'le hear no more of it.

Ev. Nay pray.

Pam. Not I I swear,——
Chide me! who have liv'd like a Saint here, and
not toucht a Wench to day!   (*Exit.*

Ev. But tarry a little.

Dio. No, let him go, I see
he's forfeited to vice and debauchery
beyond redemption; and such as he,
when vice is once turn'd nature, ne're repent,
till they find their shame, or feel their punishment
{ *Exeunt.*

Enter Filena and Amaranthe meeting.

The Scene, a Landskip or Paisage.

Fi. Amaranthe,——well met,
I've sought you all about,
And co'd not rest until I'de found you out;
You know, whilst you and I the other day

E 4   In

In yonder Mead, beheld our young Lambs play,
One of them (stragling from the rest) we spy'd
Fell down, stretcht forth its tender limbs, and dy'd
In as short time as I've been telling t'ye,
And wondring what the reason of't shu'd be,
You said 'twas with eating
a venomous herb grew there.

Am. 'Tis true,——what then?

Fi. You know besides how here,
where Love is even the vital air we breath,
and its privation consequently death;
depriv'd once of our Love, 'tis lawful for us to
despair and dye.

Am. Whither tends this discourse I wonder?

Fi. Now *Amaranthe*,
I must entreat of thee one courtesie.

Am. What need you with so many circumstances
intreat her whom you may command?
What is't?

Fi. 'Tis, that thou'dst shew me this same slye
And subtle Thief, that so insensibly
Does steal us from our selves, the lookers on
Do scarce perceive w'are going, till w'are gone.

Am. And why
wo'd you know this?

Fi. Onely for curiosity.

Am. Take heed, take heed *Filena*, it is no
Good curiosity to desire to know
Such dangerous secrets, as we well may say,

Their

Love's Kingdom. 57

Their ignorance does no harm, their knowledge
   may.

  Fi. See *Amaranthe* how unkinde th'art grown !
Wo'dft all my fecrets know, but tell me none :
But now to fatisfie your curiofity,
In plainer terms, know I'm refolv'd to dye ;
And having heard how death's a bitter cup,
To tell thee true, before I drink it up,
I'de fweeten it fo, as though the Fates do pleafe,
That I fhu'd live in pain, I'de dye with eafe.

  Am. How, you dye ! now the Gods forbid !

  Fi. No, no,
Thou art deceiv'd ; for *Amaranthe* know,
They are fo good, as when 'tis mifery
For us to live, I'me fure they'd have us dye.

  Am. But think, think what death is.

  Fi. What is it more,
then going to reft when we are weary, or
fleep when we'd reft.

  Am. I grant you, when w'are dead
Death is like reft, and th' grave but like our bed ;
But if we chance to finde unreft there, thên
As we lye down, can we rife up agen ?

  Fi. What is in t'other life, I cannot tell ;
But what there is in this, I know fo well,
As I'me refolv'd to dye ; fpare then your pain
To feek to hinder me, for 'tis in vain :——
There's but one way to live, but nature ha's
Provided us to dye a thoufand wayes ;

                              And

And hinder us from living every one
Can do, but hinder us from dying none.
   Am. I must take some other way to hinder her,
                                            (*Aside.*
For this but makes her long for death the more.
And for the way that she ha's chose to dye,
Unknown to her, I know a remedy :———
Well then, since you are so resolv'd, I'le shew
You this venomous herb, upon condition you
Let me ha'th' tempering it, to make't so sweet,
You even shall be enamour'd with taste of it.
  Fi. On any condition *Amaranthe* I'le dye,
But on no condition live in misery;
Life is not worth it, and
For noble spirits 'tis brave necessity,
When they can't honourably live, to dye;
Whilst to ignoble ones the Gods do give
For punishment, dishonourably to live.   *Exeunt.*
                                     (*Enter Philander.*
  Phi. Since no where we a constant woman finde,
But all light and wavering as the winde;
And there is no woman in all this wide
Circumference true, but she was never try'd!
Why shu'd I grieve as 'twere my fate alone,
What's common I perceive to every one?
But these are thoughts unworthy her and me,
For 'tis not hers, but my inconstancy;
If I can think her false, when I do know
Falshood wo'd even be truth, if she were so:
                                          And

Love's Kingdom. 59

And nature of things quite change, rather then she
What she has been, shu'd ever cease to be.

(*Enter* Palemon.

Pal. Oh fortunate *Palemon*! and the more,
The more unfortunate thou wert before!
And happy pains, happy affliction!
From which such pleasure and such joys do come!
Now I perceive there's none can better tell
What heaven is, then who first have past through hell.——
Methinks great conquerors who in triumph come
charg'd with the spoils of conquerd nations home
Are but the Types of me, who in triumph go
To th' Temple to enjoy *Bellinda* now. *Exiturus*

Phi. Death! If I can suffer this,
I shall deserve it:——Pray stay Sir,
for you have another victory to gain,
and enemy (I'de have you know)
to overcome, before you triumph so!

Pal. What victory d'ye mean, what enemy?

Phi. Why, I my self and the victory over me;
for know, *Bellinda*'s mine, and I her Lover.

Pal. You! did you not say you were her brother?

Phi. I, but that was onely a disguise put on,
to hide what then was fit shu'd not be known.

Pal. Why this does take all faith away from you;
For eith'r 'twas true or false you said before;
If true, why then 'tis false you tell me now;
If false, there's no believing of you more.

Phi.

Phi. This fine Dilemma wo'd serve prettily
Ith' School, but not ith' Field; where it must be
Somewhat of finer temper then your words
Must make *Bellinda* yours, I mean our Swords.
(Layes hand on's Sword.

Pal. I pray Sir hold, and e're you go so far,
consider but a little where we are,
here in *Love's Kingdom,* in a peaceful place,
where never any strife or quarrel was,
but onely loving ones.

Phi. And is not ours for Love too?

Pal. If it be, let Love decide it, are you content
to put it to his Tribunal and Arbitrement?

Phi. That's a way poor, and low spirits findes,
This is the Tribunal and Arbitrement of mighty
   mindes; *(Draws.*
'Twere folly in me to refer my Cause
Unto my enemies Tribunal and Laws.

Pal. Fortune as well as Love's your enemy,
Of her as well as Love you fear'd shu'd be.

Phi. For Love already he's declar'd my foe,
What Fortune yet may do, I do not know;
I'le try at least, my comfort is I can
Not be in worse condition then I am;
Cast down so low, it is not in the power
Of Love, or Fortune, e're to cast me lower.
(Enter Polydor.

Pol. What's here? —a quarrel tow'rds!
Our peace disturb'd, and their offensive Swords
          Th'

Love's Kingdom.

Th' uncivil Arbitrers of civil strife,
Already drawn, threatning each others life:
Our guards,— where are they there? *Exit hastily.*
  Phi. We are discry'd,
Before they come, our quarrel let's decide.
  Pal. Do, and you'l see how they but bluntly fight,
Who first consider not their Causes right;
Whilst those who well consider it before,
Have but their courages whetted by't the more,
  Phi. And unto me considering is but like
The weak opposing of some bank or dike
Unto some torrents rage, which more y'oppose,
more raging and impetuous it grows. *(They fight*
    (Enter Polydor with Guards, and parts them.
  Pol. Hold, hold, I charge you in Loves name, or else
We are to seize your weapons and your selves.
  Phi. What violence is this?
  Pol. Your self's the cause,
who first have violate Loves peaceful Laws.
  Phi. Then in Loves Kingdom here shall Lovers be
Depriv'd both of their Loves and Liberty?
  Pol. What Love d'ye mean?
  Phi. Bellinda, who is my betroathed.
  Pol. How! she your betroathed!
  Phi. I, all *Crete* can witness it.
  Pol. If this be so,

                    y'ave

y'ave too much witness here already, and you
've discovered a secret, which now 'tis known,
May prove *Bellinda*'s ruine and your own.

  Pal. O heavens!—now I remember me
by another Law, who e're doth falsifie
the sacred Oath, are instantly to dye,
sacrific'd to th' offended Deity:
But e're it comes to that, my life shall pay
the forfeiture of hers.

  Pol. Come let's away,
Palemon, you've your chamber for prison;
you Sir, must along with me unto
Theotimus to be examin'd.

  Pal. I obey you.

  Phi. And I obey necessity.   (*Exeunt.*
                               (*Manet Palemon.*

  Pal. VVell Fortune, thou giddy Goddess,
if *Bellinda* be to dye,
And thou hast onely rais'd me up so high,
To cast me down with greater force, I'le fall
So gallantly and bravely, yet as all
Shall say at least, how e're unfortunate
Palemon yet deserv'd a better fate.

    (Enter *Amaranthe* in haste with other *Nymphs.*

  Am. Run,—run, and seek her all about,
or she's but dead; and when y'ave found her out,
bring me word presently, as you love her life.—
VVas never a more unfortunate maid and wife?
                     (*Exeunt Nymphs several wayes.*
                                    Pal.

Love's Kingdom.

Pal. What busie haste is this.

Am. What are you there?
flye, flye *Palemon*, or the Nymphs will tear
you in pieces.

Pal. Why?

Am. For killing the gentlest maid
eye ever saw, or *Cyprus* ever had;

Pal. What maid d'ye mean?

Am. Filena.

Pal. Why! is she dead?

Am. Dead, dead, kill'd by your cruelty
And see poor soul what she does write to me,

She reads.

Filena's Letter.

Pardon me Amaranthe,
for having taken the poison unknown unto you,
and deceiv'd you once in my life,
rather then you shu'd deceive me in my death.
Commend me to Palemon, *and tell him,*
that as I liv'd in hope of his love,
so now I dye for despair of it:
and let him after I am dead but wish me rest,
and I shall rest in peace. ———

FILENA.

Am. And so I hope thou do'st
fair gentle maid, or th' Gods shu'd else be most
unkinde and cruel, shu'd they not to thee grant
that rest in death, which thou in life didst want.——
Now you who for cruelty surpass

The

The cruel'st savage Beast that ever was;
Some Tyger bore thee sure, or thou wert bred
With Tygers milk at least, and nourished:
If thou who art the cause of all canst hear
This, and not vent a sigh, nor shed a tear.

Pal. As for my sighing and my weeping, that
Is an expression too effeminate;
Onely for single losses: such as mine
Requires expressions far more masculine:
Where grief and sorrows are redoubled,
For dying *Bellinda,* and *Filena* dead. (*Exit.*

Am. What's that? *Bellinda* dying does he say?
Sure Love and death have chang'd their darts to day,
and there's some Planet reigns will kill us all,
but I forget *Filena.*

Enter a Nymph.

Oh now I shall
hear news of her——well have you found her?

Mel. No,
but *Lydia* sayes sh'ave trac't her footsteps to
the sacred Grove.

Am. Take a cruise presently
Of purest water then, and follow me;
Yet there is hope I may retard her fate,
And save her life, which Love does make her hate.

Finis Actus quarti.

A C-

ACTUS 5.

Filena Sola.

The Scene, a Wood or Boscage.

Filena.

THe poison now's arriv'd unto my heart,
The place assign'd where life and I must part,
And where I must resign my latest breath,
Then farewel life, and welcome sweetest death;
To prisoners freedom, to the weary rest,
Comfort to th' sad, and ease to the opprest:
Who'd then indure such worlds of miseries,
When life's but pain, and death no more but this?
Now, now I dye, yet Love lives in me still,

Falls.

As if what Love does wound, Death durst not kill.
Who doubt then whether thou immortal art,
(O mighty Love) could they but see my heart,
And bosom here, where thou canst never dye,
It would assert thy immortality.

Enter Pamphilus.

Pam. Bless me!
amongst what a generation of Nymphs
am I fallen here, who are all so precise and pure,
as when they come but where men are, they take
the wind of 'um, for fear of being got with child,
as Spanish Ginnets are, and when they go away

F   brush

Clo. And mine,

Mel. And all of ours to boot. *(Enter Palemon.*

Pol. O *Palemon* welcome, I sent for you
by order of *Theotimus*, to let you know
strange news of *Bellinda*.

Pal. I fear I am but too
familiar with it already. *(they whisper.*

Am. See, she begins to stir,
And opens her eyes; I told you their fair light
Was but ecclipst and not extinguisht quite.

Pol. Then you may let him go;

Pam. Marry,
and I'le be gone then as fast as I can,
and flye the land too, before I'le be put in such
a fright again. *(Exit.*

Fil. Where am I? in what Region of the dead!
not in hell sure, for there
are far more horrid visions then are here;
nor yet in heaven, for there agen
are far more glorious ones; where am I'then?

An. She thinks she's dead still.

Fil. Ha, *Palemon* here! nay then I see
Love takes delight still in tormenting me, (Hell,
And there's some middle place twixt Heaven and
Where wretched Lovers, such as I, do dwell;
Where sh'ud I go to flye the sight of men,
And where to flye Loves fires and arrows, when
Where e're I go, just like the wounded Dear,
I flye in vain, that which I carry here. *(Exit.*

Am. Go

Love's Kingdom.

Am. Go follow her,
and look carefully unto her,
Her wandring minde you'l see will come anon
unto its self, when her amazement's gone.
　Pal. Whate're it be, methinks there's somewhat here
Whispers remorse, and chides me (as it were)
For my unkindness, and stern cruelty
Unto this Nymph, who thus wo'd dye for me;
But as loud windes won't let us hear the soft
And gentle voice of others; so the thought
Of dying for *Bellinda*, will not let
Me hear its voice nor hearken to it yet.
Enter Diophantes.
　Dio. O noble youth! whose famous memory
Shall never be forgot, or ever be
remembred without praise.
　Pal. What news brings *Diophantes*,
he's so transported with it?
　Dio. That, which had I a thousand tongues to tell,
Or you a thousand ears to hear, wou'd well
Deserve them all.—Soon as 'twas rumored,
Bellinda must dye for having falsified
The sacred Oath: but this stranger instantly
Offered himself with such alacrity
to dye for her; as Love
ne're gain'd so glorious a victory, nor
ever so triumpht over death before,

Pal. Oh

Pal. Oh me! if this be so, I shall become
th' derision and the scorn of every one;
and was his offer accepted?

Dio. That you know
by th' Laws here co'd not be refus'd him.

Pal. How!
Ha's he prevented me? but do I stand
Senseless and stupid, as I were dead here,—and
Had not a life to lose as well as he?
No generous stranger whosoe're thou be,
Since thou wert born my Rival, thou shalt prove
I'le rival thee in Death as well as Love. (*Exit.*

Pol. I fear the event of this!

Am. And so do I;
But wherefore is *Bellinda* doom'd to dye?

Pol. For perjury and falshood, whilst she swore,
She lov'd one here, being betroath'd before
unto that stranger there.

Am. All thât may be
Without forswearing yet and perjury;
For what if he she swore she lov'd be he
she was betroath'd unto?

Pol. That cannot be,
For she was in the sacred Cell 'tis clear,
Long time before he e're arrived here;
In Sequestration, separated from
Society of all, mean time her tongue
Charm'd silent, and eyes blinded as they were,
How co'd she see or know that he was here?

Dio.

Dio. Are you convinced yet?

Am. No, not always they
Convinced are, who know not what to say;
For my part until farther proof shall shew
Her guilty, I shall ne're believe her so:
For just as Images in Tapestry
Do all appear distorted and awry,
Until they're fully explicate, and then
We see they appear all right and streight agen;
So shê we now think guilty, we may finde
Innocent perhaps, when she explains her minde.

Pol. Pray heaven she may! mean time let us go see
This stranger, who shall ever honour'd be
Alive and dead; and be all Lovers boast,
and honour to Love's Kingdom.

Am. And that most
deservedly, for never any yet
For truly loving did more honour get;
Nor ever any whilst the world lasts, or
There's Lovers in the world shall e're get more.
{ *Exeunt.*

Enter Theotimus, Chorus of Musicians, Philander led to Sacrifice crown'd Victim-wise, Youths and Virgins with baskets of flowers strewing the way, &c. Evander.

The. Go noble youth, who does in dying prove
Death, who has power o're all, has none o're Love
And shews to th' world, that who refuse to give

Their lives for honour ne're deserv'd to live:
Go take with thee this consolation,
You lose a life that easily wo'd be gone;
But gain one by't, when thousand years are past,
And thousand other lives, shall always last;
And though you might have longer liv'd, yet know,
You ne're could dye more gloriously then now;
To have all our Youths and Virgins strew
With flowers all the way you go,
With Roses and with Mirtle Boughs
Adorning your victorious browes;
And singing with triumphant Song
Your praises as you go along.
            Chorus sings.
Thus shall he ever honour'd be,
Who dyes for Love and Constancy;
And thus be ever prais'd, who dyes
Love's Martyr, and his Sacrifice.
The. And if alive you thus are honoured,
Much more you shall be after you are dead;
If such as you can e're be said to dye,
By whose noble example and memory,
A thousand Lovers when y'are dead and gone,
Shall spring up in the world instead of one;
Who every year on pilgrimage shall come
To honour your dead ashes in their tomb,
Seeing whose votive gifts and offerings,
The greatest and the mightiest of Kings,

                                       In

In envying you, and wishing them their own,
Shall for your tomb gladly exchange their throne

Chorus sings.
*Thus shall he ever honour'd be,
Who dyes for Love and Constancy;
And thus be ever prais'd, who dyes
Love's Martyr, and his Sacrifice.*

*Enter Palemon, Diophantes, Polydor, Amaranthe,
&c. following.*

Pal. Justice, Justice, Sir.
The. For what? or against whom?
Pal. Against that stranger there,
who'd rob me of the honour and happiness
of dying for *Bellinda*.
Phi. He's more unjust then I,
who 'as rob'd me of the honour and happiness
of living for her, and now won't let me dye.
Pal. As if no rocks nor seas, nor flames there were
Nor other wayes of dying, but for her?
Chuse any of them you please, your choice is free,
Onely dying for her belongs to me.
Phi. You may live for her, what wo'd you more?
were I
So happy as you, who's fit for me shu'd dye.
Pal. You talk as if there were no life to come,
No blessed Shades nor no *Elizium*;
Where those who have been Lovers here possess
Eternity of joyes and happiness.

Phi.

Phi. Heaven is my witness I ne're think upon
The joyes and pleasures of *Elizium,*
Nor any joyes or pleasures whatsoe're
But that of dying and suffering for her.
  Ev. How like two towering Hawks they mount and soar,
Love never flew so high a flight before!
  Dio. There'l be no end of this.
  Pol. Peace, let them alone,
Greater example of Love was never shown!
  The. Then let *Bellinda* come, and sentence give
Whether of them shu'd dye, and whether live;
Are you content?
  Pal. I am.
  Phi. And so am I
ready for her either to live or dye.
The. Bring her forth thên, with all the ceremonies
requisite in so dire a Sacrifice,
All the Nymphs in mourning accompaning her,
The fatal Axe and Executioner
Before her, and (the whilst they go along)
The *Chorus* singing of her Funeral Song.

  The Song, sung whilst the Nymphs put on
       their mourning Veils.

Oh! Oh! Oh! Oh!
Never was there greater woe,
Let us all the habits borrow,
And the face of grief and sorrow;

                        Who'd

Who'd not spare a sigh nor tear
From all mishaps to spend it here!

Enter Bellinda veil'd, brought in by Polydor, the Popa, or sacred Executioner before her, all the Nymphs weeping, &c.

Ev. Wherefore this ceremony, since she's not to
Di. Onely for terrour and formality.   (dye?
Th. Come,— thus I unveil thy eyes, that thou mayest see
Unto what misery and calamity
T'hast brought thy self and us, and thus uncharm
Thy tongue, the fatal cause of all this harm.
Bel. What means these sable weeds and mourning chear?
Whilst not a face but wears death's Livery here!
Th. 'Tis all for thee, (unhappy Nymph) put on,
That thou shud'st dye so untimely, and so young.
Bel. I understand you not, nor can I fear
Death, whilst my dearest life, *Philander's* here.
Pal. How's this?
(She goes to embrace Philander, and he turns away
Ev. This is more strange then t'other!
Bel. Ha!
Philander prove unkinde! nay, then away
With the fatal Axe and Executioner,
And all these deadly preparations here,
They need not now; one unkinde look or two
Of his, can kill me sooner then they can do.

The.

The. It is thy falshood and perfidity,
(Unfortunate Nymph) that kills thee, and not he;
Whilst falsly and perfidiously you swore,
You lov'd one here, being betroath'd before
unto another.

Bel. How! I ne're did swear,
That I lov'd any but *Philander* here!

Pal. Oh killing declaration!

The. That cant't be.
For as for him, all *Cyprus* knows that he
Arriv'd not here, till after you were inclos'd
Ith' sacred Cell, and separated from
All conversation; ith' mean time your tongue
Charm'd silent, and Eyes blinded as they were,
How could you see or know that he was here?

Bel. Love is a fire, and there needs no eye,
But onely heat to tell when fire is nigh;
And Lovers by their glowing bosoms know
When those are near they love: but lest this now
Might seem too mystical, to make't more clear;
As in the Temple I came forth to swear,
I heard his voice, and swounding instantly
For joy to hear it, whilst officiously
They lifted up my Veil to give me air,
I glanc'd my eyes aside, and saw him there,

The. Can any thing be more clear?

Pol. Or any more
Deceiv'd in judgement, then we were before?

Am. Did I not tell you she was innocent, I?

Bel.

Bel. Yet can you doubt my faith and constancy?
Phi. No, but I doubt whet'r yet I wake or dream,
My extasie and joy is so extream. (*They embrace.*
 Ev. See how they stand so ravisht with delight,
And so transported each in t'others sight,
'T can scarcely be conceiv'd by humane breast,
Much less by humane tongue can be exprest.
 Th. Disturb them not,—& now a word with you *Palemon*.
 Fi. Now Love grant my hopes be true.
 Bel. Co'd you be jealous of me?
 Phi. Dearest know,
I shu'd not love so dearly as I do,
Were I not jealous; for jealousie
'S but scorching of Loves fire, and he shu'd be
But a cold Lover, who sometimes at least
Felt not a little of it in his breast.
 The. Come, come, I here command you to restore
That heart unto her, you took from her before;
For all the Isle knows 'twas *Filena*, who
Enkindled the first sparks of Love in you;
Till (haplesly for both) *Bellinda* came,
And after rais'd those sparks unto a flame,
And holy Vestals ne're with greater care
Preserve their fires, then we Loves fire's air,
Enkindling one straight in anothers room.
 Pal. In tepid hearths fires kindle not so soon.
 The. Call not that tepid, where late such a fire
Did burn, ne're any in *Cyprus* flamed higher.
Pal.

Pal. But Loves fires once extinguisht, leave hearts more
Tepid, and cold then e're they were before.

The. Come, don't dispute, for I'm to be obey'd,
And now but look upon this gentle maid,
And tell me truly, did you ever see
A fairer, or a sweeter Nymph then she!
One for whose love there's not a gentle Swain
In all the Land, but sighs, and sighs in vain;
And she to love you, and to love you so,
She willingly would dye for love of you:
What cleansing water, or what purging flame
Can expiate your not loving her again?

Fi. Fall all the fault on this devoted head,
Rather then blame him for't, wou'd I were dead;
'Tis my unworthiness, and no fault of his,
He does not love, if any fault there is. (mov'd

The. Yet (obstinate as you are) are you not
To love again where y'are so dearly lov'd?

Pal. These vaults and walls built 'for eternity,
Love's Temple shall be sooner mov'd then I:

The. Nay then 'tis needful we apply I see
Our utmost and extreamest remedy,
Lest the contagion o'th' example shu'd
Nourish bad humors, and corrupt the good :)
Let him to th' desart Island straight be led
Whither all Loves Rebels are banished.

Pal. Unto what place so e're I am confin'd,
I may change place, but cannot change my mind;
But

But stay! what sudden earthquakes this I feel,
Makes the walls totter, and foundations reel
o'th' Temple here!

The. 'Tis well, 'tis a good sign,
Love who moves stones will move that heart of
 (thine,
More hard then they—and see O wondrous sight!
The Temples fill'd with unaccustom'd light;
And love with flaming brand amidst it flyes,
Illuminating with it all the skies:
Now (rebel as thou art) thou soon shalt know
Whether Love's God have any power or no.

Pal. Just as some gentle gale does fan the fire,
There's somewhat here within that does inspire
My breast, and now't increases more and more,
Till that which onely was a spark before
Does by degrees so mighty a flame become,
As I am all but one incendium!
O Love, to whom all bosoms must submit,
I feel thy mighty hand, and reverence it!

The. Just so *Phæbus*, the Delphick God inspires,
The *Pythonesses* breast with sacred fires,
Onely the God of Love more mildly burns,
And 'stead of raging unto sweetness turns.

Chorus sings.

So gentle Love does all command
In fire and water, air and land,
And all with his commands inspire
In Land and water, aire and fire.

Pal. And

Pal. And can you pardon me?

Fi. I can pardon any thing
in my *Palemon*, but onely his doubting
whether I can or no. And for the rest,
Account my self by *Love* most highly blest,
(Who payes debts best the longer he forbears)
T'have all my morning sighs and evening tears,
My daily griefs and nightly sorrows past,
Rewarded thus abundantly at last.

 Pal. My dear *Filena*.   } *They*
 Fi. My dearest, dearest *Palemon*. } *embrace.*

 The. Enough, enough, leave your embraces till
At fitter season you may take your fill
Of such delicious pleasures and contents,
Such sweet delights, such joyes and ravishments,
No heart can e're conceive, no tongue express
The thousandth part of their deliciousness.——
        (*To Phi. and Bel.*
Now see and wonder, these are Lovers too,
This is the least of miracles Love can do.

 Phi. Noble *Palemon*, I congratulate
Your and the fair *Filena's* happy fate:

 Pal. And I, noble *Philander*, rejoyce no less
At your and fair *Bellinda's* happiness.

 The. Never was more abundant joy, and now
To th' paradice of happy Lovers go, (*prove*
Where with redoubled flames Love's God does
Whose hearts are most capacious of love:
And then with all becoming rites and state,
        When

When once your marriages are celebrate;
Philander you, and fair *Bellinda* may
At your best pleasure either go or stay. (*Exeunt.*

Manet Evander, to whom Pamphilus *enters.*

Pam. And what shall we do?
Evan. I for my part, since
there's so much joy and happiness
in marriage, resolve first to go home
and dispose of all I have, and after come
and marry here.
Pam. Promise you so won't I,
if there be no wenches
nor wenching businesses here,
it is no place for me; wherefore my word is,
Come here no more.
Ev. And mine is, *Come agen.*
Pam. I'm sure I shall have the greatest part
of my opinion.
Ev. And I all the nobler and the better——
And now let's see which number is the greater.

FINIS.

G *Filena's*

Filena's Song, of the commutation of *Love*'s and *Death*'s Darts.

In the narrative Style.

Love and Death o'th' way once meeting,
Having past a friendly greeting:
Sleep their weary Eye-lids closing,
Lay them down themselves reposing.
Love whom divers cares molested,
Could not sleep, but while Death rested,
All in haste away he postes him,
But his haste full dearly costs him:
For it chanc't that going to sleeping
Both did give their darts in keeping
Unto Night, who Errors mother,
Blindly knowing not one from t'other,
Gave Love Death's, and ne're perceiv'd it,
Whilst as blindely Love receiv'd it;
Since which time their Darts confounding,
Love now kills instead of wounding:
Death our hearts with sweetness filling,
Gently wounds instead of killing.

An-

Another Song.

Elia weeps, and those fair eyes
Which sparkling Diamonds were before,
Whose precious brightness none could prize,
Dissolves into a pearly showre.

Celia smiles, and straight does render
Her fair Eyes Diamonds again,
Which after shine with greater splendor,
As the Sun does after rain.

Now if the reason you would know,
Why Pearls and Diamonds fall and rise;
Their prices just go high or low,
As they are worn in Celia's Eyes.

FINIS.

A Short
DISCOURSE
OF THE
English Stage.

A SHORT DISCOURSE OF THE Englifh Stage.

To his Excellency, the Lord Marquefs of NEWCASTLE.

My Noble Lord,

I Send your Excellency here a fhort Difcourfe of the *Englifh Stage*, (which if you pleas'd you could far better treat of then my felf) but before I begin it, I will fpeak a word or two of thôfe of other Countreys.

About the midft of the laft Century, Playes, after a long difcontinuance, and civil death in a manner, began to be reviv'd again, firft in *Italy* by *Guarino*, *Taffo*, *de Porta*, and others; and afterwards in *Spain* by *Lopes de Vega*, the French beginning later by reafon of their Civil Wars, Cardinal *Richlieu* being the first that brought them into that Vouge and Esteem as now they are; well knowing how much the Acting noble and heroick Playes, conferr'd to the instilling a noble and heroick Spirit into the Nation. For ûs, we began before them, and if since they seem to have out-stript us, 'tis because our Stage ha's stood at a stand this many years; nor may we doubt, but now we shall soon out-strip them again, if we hold on but as we begin. Of the Dutch I speak nothing, because they are but slow, and follow other Nations onely afar off: But to return unto our present subject.

Playes (which so flourisht amongst the Greeks, and afterwards amongst the Romans) were almost wholly abolished when their Empire was first converted to Christianity, and their Theaters, together with their Temples, for the most part, demolished as Reliques of Paganisme, some few onely reserved and dedicate to the service of the True God, as they had been to their false gods before; from which time to the last Age, they Acted nothing here, but Playes of the holy Scripture, 'or Saints Lives; and that without any certain Theaters or set Companies, till about the beginning of Queen *Elizabeths* Reign, they began here to assemble into Companies, and set up Theaters, first in the City, (as in the Innyards of the *Cross-Keyes*, and *Bull* in *Grace*

and

of the English Stage.

and *Bishops-Gate Street* at this day is to be seen) till that Fanatick Spirit which then began with the Stage, and after ended with the Throne, banisht them thence into the Suburbs, as after they did the Kingdom, in the beginning of our Civil Wars. In which time, Playes were so little incompatible with Religion, and the Theater with the Church, as on Week-dayes after Vespers, both the Children of the Chappel and St. *Pauls*, Acted Playes, the one in *White-Friers*, the other behinde the Convocation-house in *Pauls*, till people growing more precise, and Playes more licentious, the Theatre of *Pauls* was quite suppreft, and that of the Children of the Chappel, converted to the use of the Children of the Revels.

In this time were Poets and Actors in their greatest flourish, *Johnson*, *Shakespear*, with *Beaumont* and *Fletcher* their Poets, and *Field* and *Burbidge* their Actors.

For Playes, *Shakespear* was one of the first, who inverted the Dramatick Stile, from dull History to quick Comedy, upon whom *Johnson* refin'd; as *Beaumont* and *Fletcher* first writ in the Heroick way, upon whom *Suckling* and others endeavoured to refine agen; one saying wittily of his *Aglaura*, that 'twas full of fine flowers, but they seem'd rather stuck, then growing there; as another of *Shakespear's* writings, that 'twas

a

A short Discourse

a fine Garden, but it wanted weeding.

There are few of our English Playes (excepting onely some few of *Johnsons*) without some faults or other; and if the French have fewer then our English, 'tis because they confine themselves to narrower limits, and consequently have less liberty to erre.

The chief faults of ours, are our huddling too much matter together, and making them too long and intricate; we imagining we never have intrigue enough, till we lose our selves and Auditors, who shu'd be led in a Maze, but not a Mist; and through turning and winding wayes, but so still, as they may finde their way at last.

A good Play shu'd be like a good stuff, closely and evenly wrought, without any breakes, thrums, or loose ends in 'um, or like a good Picture well painted and designed; the Plot or Contrivement, the Design, the Writing, the Coloris, and Counterplot, the Shaddowings, with other Embellishments: or finally, it shu'd be like a well contriv'd Garden, cast into its Walks and Counterwalks, betwixt an Alley and a Wilderness, neither too plain, nor too confus'd. Of all Arts, that of the Dramatick Poet is the most difficult and most subject to censure; for in all others, they write onely of some particular subject, as the Mathematician of Mathematicks, or Philosopher of Phi-

of the English Stage.

Philosophy; but in that, the Poet must write of every thing, and every one undertakes to judge of it.

A Dramatick Poet is to the Stage as a Pilot to the Ship; and to the Actors, as an Architect to the Builders, or Master to his Schollars: he is to be a good moral Philosopher, but yet more learned in Men then Books. He is to be a wise, as well as a witty Man, and a good man, as well as a good Poet; and I'de allow him to be so far a good fellow too, to take a chearful cup to whet his wits, so he take not so much to dull 'um, and whet 'um quite away.

To compare our English Dramatick Poets together (without taxing them) *Shakespear* excelled in a natural Vein, *Fletcher* in Wit, and *Johnson* in Gravity and ponderousness of Style; whose onely fault was, he was too elaborate; and had he mixt less erudition with his Playes, they had been more pleasant and delightful then they are. Comparing him with *Shakespear*, you shall see the difference betwixt Nature and Art; and with *Fletcher*, the difference betwixt Wit and Judgement: Wit being an exuberant thing, like *Nilus*, never more commendable then when it overflowes; but Judgement a stayed and reposed thing, alwayes containing it self within its bounds and limits.

Beaumont and *Fletcher* were excellent in their kinde, but they often err'd against *Decorum*, seldom

A short Discourse

dom representing a valiant man without somewhat of the *Braggadoccio*, nor an honourable woman without somewhat of *Dol Common* in her: to say nothing of their irreverent representing Kings persons on the Stage, who shu'd never be represented, but with Reverence: Besides, *Fletcher* was the first who introduc't that witty obscenity in his Playes, which like poison infused in pleasant liquor, is alwayes the more dangerous the more delightful. And here to speak a word or two of Wit, it is the spirit and quintessence of speech, extracted out of the substance of the thing we speak of, having nothing of the superfice, or dross of words (as clenches, quibbles, gingles, and such like trifles have) it is that, in pleasant and facetious discourse, as Eloquence is in grave and serious; not learnt by Art and Precept, but Nature and Company. 'Tis in vain to say any more of it; for if I could tell you what it were, it would not be what it is; being somewhat above expression, and such a volatil thing, as 'tis altogether as volatil to describe.

It was the happiness of the Actors of those Times to have such Poets as these to instruct them, and write for them; and no less of those Poets to have such docile and excellent Actors to Act their Playes, as a *Field* and *Burbidge*; of whom we may say, that he was a delightful *Proteus*, so wholly transforming himself into his Part,

and

of the English Stage.

and putting off himself with his Cloathes, as he never (not so much as in the Tyring-house) assum'd himself again until the Play was done: there being as much difference betwixt him and one of our common Actors, as between a Ballad-singer who onely mouths it, and an excellent singer, who knows all his Graces, and can artfully vary and modulate his Voice, even to know how much breath he is to give to every syllable. He had all the parts of an excellent Orator, (animating his words with speaking, and Speech with Action) his Auditors being never more delighted then when he spake, nor more sorry then when he held his peace; yet even then, he was an excellent Actor still, never falling in his Part when he had done speaking; but with his looks and gesture, maintaining it still unto the heighth, he imagining *Age quod agis*, onely spoke to him: so as those who call him a Player do him wrong, no man being less idle then he, whose whole life is nothing else but action, with only this difference from other mens, that as what is but a Play to them, is his Business; so their business is but a play to him.

Now, for the difference betwixt our Theaters and those of former times, they were but plain and simple, with no other Scenes, nor Decorations of the Stage, but onely old Tapestry, and the Stage strew'd with Rushes, (with their Habits accordingly) whereas ours now for

cost

A short Discourse

cost and ornament are arriv'd to the heighth of Magnificence; but that which makes our Stage the better, makes our Playes the worse perhaps, they striving now to make them more for sight, then hearing; whence that solid joy of the interior is lost, and that benefit which men formerly receiv'd from Playes, from which they seldom or never went away, but far better and wiser then they came.

The Stage being a harmless and innocent Recreation; where the minde is recreated and delighted, and that *Ludus Literarum*, or School of good Language and Behaviour, that makes Youth soonest Man, and man soonest good and vertuous, by joyning example to precept, and the pleasure of seeing to that of hearing. Its chiefest end is, to render Folly ridiculous, Vice odious, and Vertue and Noblenesse so amiable and lovely, as, every one shu'd be delighted and enamoured with it; from which when it deflects; as, *corruptio optimi pessima:* of the best it becomes the worst of Recreations. And this his Majesty well understood, when after his happy Restauration, he took such care to purge it from all vice and obscenity; and would to God he had found all bodies and humours as apt and easie to be purg'd and reform'd as that.

For Scenes and Machines they are no new invention, our Masks and some of our Playes in
former

of the English Stage.

former times (though not so ordinary) having had as good or rather better then any we have now.

They are excellent helps of imagination, most grateful deceptions of the sight, and graceful and becoming Ornaments of the Stage, transporting you easily without lassitude from one place to another; or rather by a kinde of delightful Magick, whilst you sit still, does bring the place to you. Of this curious Art the *Italians* (this latter age) are the greatest masters, the *French* good proficients, and we in *England* onely Schollars and Learners yet, having proceeded no further then to bare painting, and not arriv'd to the stupendious wonders of your great Ingeniers, especially not knowing yet how to place our Lights, for the more advantage and illuminating of the Scenes.

And thus much suffices it briefly to have said of all that concerns our Modern Stage, onely to give others occasion to say more.

FINIS.